Tailoring Deterrence for China in Space

KRISTA LANGELAND, DEREK GROSSMAN

Prepared for the OSD
Approved for public release; distribution unlimited

NATIONAL SECURITY RESEARCH DIVISION

For more information on this publication, visit **www.rand.org/t/RRA943-1**.

About RAND

The RAND Corporation is a research organization that develops solutions to public policy challenges to help make communities throughout the world safer and more secure, healthier and more prosperous. RAND is nonprofit, nonpartisan, and committed to the public interest. To learn more about RAND, visit www.rand.org.

Research Integrity

Our mission to help improve policy and decisionmaking through research and analysis is enabled through our core values of quality and objectivity and our unwavering commitment to the highest level of integrity and ethical behavior. To help ensure our research and analysis are rigorous, objective, and nonpartisan, we subject our research publications to a robust and exacting quality-assurance process; avoid both the appearance and reality of financial and other conflicts of interest through staff training, project screening, and a policy of mandatory disclosure; and pursue transparency in our research engagements through our commitment to the open publication of our research findings and recommendations, disclosure of the source of funding of published research, and policies to ensure intellectual independence. For more information, visit www.rand.org/about/principles.

RAND's publications do not necessarily reflect the opinions of its research clients and sponsors.

Published by the RAND Corporation, Santa Monica, Calif.
© 2021 RAND Corporation
RAND® is a registered trademark.

Library of Congress Cataloging-in-Publication Data is available for this publication.
ISBN: 978-1-9774-0703-0

Cover: *Long March 5 Y2 by* 篁竹水声

About This Report

The United States has become increasingly reliant on space-based capabilities for its own economic prosperity, for the defense of both the United States and its allies, and for facilitating cross-domain joint military operations. At the same time, China has come to assign a great strategic importance to space superiority and may view U.S. activity in space as an obstacle to achieving space supremacy.[1] As a result, the U.S. government views the protection of these capabilities and the deterrence of any activity that could degrade them as vital to national security. This report examines the application of classical deterrence theory to the space domain and discusses how China's own objectives should be considered to build a tailored deterrence strategy for China in space.

The research reported here was completed in March 2021 and underwent security review with the sponsor and the Defense Office of Prepublication and Security Review before public release.

This research was conducted within the International Security and Defense Policy Center of the RAND National Security Research Division, which operates the National Defense Research Institute, a federally funded research and development center sponsored by the Office of the Secretary of Defense, the Joint Staff, the Unified

---

[1] See Pollpeter, Chase, and Heginbotham, 2017.

Combatant Commands, the Navy, the Marine Corps, the defense agencies, and the defense intelligence enterprise.

For more information on the RAND International Security and Defense Policy Center, see www.rand.org/nsrd/isdp or contact the director (contact information is provided on the webpage).

Contents

Summary

China has set out ambitious goals in space. Perceiving space as a domain of strategic importance, it is seeking dominance there. According to primary source documents, the United States is perceived as being an obstacle to these goals, and because of this, China is incentivized to develop and deploy capabilities that could interfere with space-based capabilities of the United States. For this reason, the United States is particularly interested in deterring China in space. While we can rely on the principles of deterrence strategy outlined in classical deterrence theory, a new strategy for space needs to be tailored to the specific context of the space domain and particular U.S. objectives and perceptions of China. Tailoring deterrence for China in space requires a consideration of both the space domain's unique characteristics and China's ambitions in this domain.

Tailored deterrence in space requires a shift from some of the ideas that shaped strategies for classical deterrence during the Cold War, particularly because the United States is moving from deterrence of a particular weapon to deterrence *in a domain*. A deterrence strategy for the space domain needs to shift from a focus on the use of nuclear weapons to targeting a wide variety of behaviors that could interfere with operations in this domain. Further, operations in the space domain may rely on capabilities outside of the space domain and thereby expand the boundaries of a space deterrence strategy across different domains. A successful deterrence strategy *tailored to China* requires an understanding of Beijing's own objectives and its ability to shape perceived gains from interfering with United States and allied space-based capabilities.

Strategic messaging is important here, and messaging for enhancing deterrence should target not only China, but also the broader global community.

The purpose of this report is to consider potential ways in which the United States, along with key allies and partners, can effectively deter China in space—that is, prevent Beijing from taking actions in space or interfering with space-based capabilities in ways that are inimical to U.S. national security interests.[1] To begin tailoring a deterrence strategy, we first discuss deterrence in the space domain, examining key tenets of deterrence and how they may or may not be relevant in space. We then start the process of tailoring deterrence for China, specifically in the space domain. As explained by deterrence experts, tailored deterrence is an extension of traditional deterrence: Whereas the latter seeks to prevent an adversary from taking an undesirable path through threat of punishment or denial, the former customizes deterrence efforts to a specific nation state.[2] Tailoring deterrence for a particular adversary specifically in the space domain requires an in-depth understanding of the adversary's objectives, its approach to deterrence, and how it perceives the credibility and cost of retaliation should deterrence fail. We begin the process of tailoring deterrence for China in space by examining Beijing's goals and approach to space deterrence from the perspective of openly available Chinese primary source materials. After highlighting and summarizing key findings from the primary source literature, we then offer several potential implications for the United States as well as allies and partners in the Indo-Pacific. Finally, we consider several potential areas for further research.

---

[1]   Our definition includes Chinese testing of capabilities that could be used against the U.S. military in the future.

[2]   For a seminal piece on tailored deterrence, see Bunn, 2007. For more recent work on tailoring deterrence, see Nakatani, forthcoming.

Acknowledgments

In this report the authors relied heavily on RAND's rich history and ongoing research of deterrence strategy in the space domain and security cooperation, and we are very grateful for insight and guidance from several of their colleagues who shared their expertise in these areas. Bruce McClintock and Steven Flanagan not only helped shape this report from the ground up, but also provided input and guidance along the way and ensured we were addressing a range of perspectives on deterrence from across the space community. Nathan Beauchamp-Mustafaga and Tristan Finazzo compiled and translated the primary source documents referenced in this report. Hannah Byrne provided important comments to help us clarify the narrative. We are grateful to our peer reviewers, James Mulvenon and Karl Mueller: Their perspectives were invaluable in helping us clarify and better address important concepts in this report. We thank Mike Spirtas for his comments and discussions on deterrence and Mike McNerney for making important connections to colleagues at the Center for Air and Space Power Strategic Studies (CASPSS) in Japan. We are extremely grateful for perspective from CASPSS on deterrence in space, and in particular, we would like to thank Colonel Kenji Minami for helping us engage with CASPSS and Captain Hiroshi Nakatani for his valuable insights on tailored deterrence.

Abbreviations

ASAT	anti-satellite
DoD	Department of Defense
PLA	People's Liberation Army of China
PLASSF	PLA Strategic Support Force
SDA	space domain awareness
USAF	United States Air Force
USSF	United States Space Force

CHAPTER ONE

The Importance of Deterring China in Space

Just over 60 years ago, the first artificial satellite was launched into space, introducing an era of technological development and political competition that has changed the way we view and utilize this domain. Space now plays a significant role not only in scientific achievement and exploration, but also in assuring security and prosperity for nations that possess and rely on assets in space. This is true particularly for the United States. Its space-based capabilities are now integral to economic prosperity, to the defense of both the United States and its allies across all domains, and to facilitating cross-domain joint military operations. Furthermore, there is a growing reliance on space-based capabilities as a source of information and support for the warfighter on the ground, as evidenced by their vital role in modern U.S. military operations in the Middle East over recent decades.[1] Because of this reliance on space-based capabilities in modern conflict, the U.S. government views the protection of these capabilities and the deterrence of any activity that could degrade them as vital to national security.

While maintaining the peaceful use of outer space is a stated goal of the international community, it is nevertheless recognized that space

---

[1] Space-based capabilities can provide operational advantages in reconnaissance, early warning, communications, navigation, and even information about weather conditions. These advantages were demonstrated during the United States' operations in the region, including Operation Desert Storm, Operation Enduring Freedom, and Operation Iraqi Freedom. See, for example, Vergun, 2021.

could become a domain of conflict.[2] A growing recognition of the potential for conflict in space is reflected in recent force structure and policy shifts in the United States. In December 2019, the National Defense Authorization Act for Fiscal Year 2020 was signed into law, creating the United States Space Force (USSF) via a significant reorganization of the U.S military.[3] The 2020 U.S. National Defense Space Strategy asserts that "space is now a distinct warfighting domain, demanding enterprise-wide changes to policies, strategies, operations, investments, capabilities, and expertise for a new strategic environment."[4]

The recognition of the potential for conflict in space is also reflected in recent shifts in Chinese force structure and policy. As China continues to modernize and professionalize the People's Liberation Army (PLA), it has become clear that Beijing prioritizes outer space as both a key enabler of terrestrial joint military operations and as a new warfighting domain. Indeed, Beijing has called space the "new commanding heights of strategic competition" and a "critical domain" for warfighting.[5] According to its 2016 space white paper, China plans to become "a space power in all respects."[6] Ultimately, Beijing plans to leverage space warfare capabilities to achieve Chinese President Xi Jinping's directives for PLA modernization to be "basically completed" by 2035 and to elevate the PLA to "world-class" status by 2050—likely meaning on par with the U.S. military.[7] Most notably, in late 2015 Xi established the PLA Strategic Support Force (PLASSF), which is charged with centralizing and conducting PLA

---

[2] The United Nations Outer Space Treaty that came into effect in October 1967 states that space should be reserved for peaceful uses. See United Nations General Assembly, 1967. Indeed, many in the space community assert that the space domain has been militarized all along, and the debate now is over its weaponization.

[3] See U.S. Congress, H.R. 2500 National Defense Authorization Act for Fiscal Year 2020.

[4] U.S. Department of Defense (DoD), 2020a.

[5] China's State Council Information Office, 2015. The "new commanding heights" description is also discussed in Lewis, 2018.

[6] China National Space Administration, 2016.

[7] Xi, 2017. For analysis of Xi's goals, see Grossman, 2019.

space operations and integrating them with cyber and electronic warfare capabilities.[8]

In addition to preparing for potential future conflict in the space domain, the United States and other leading space-faring nations continue to develop counterspace capabilities. Countries have been developing anti-satellite (ASAT) weapons for decades. The United States fired an ASM-135 missile from an F-15 fighter to destroy a solar observation satellite in 1985.[9] In 2007, China demonstrated an ability to destroy an object in space by conducting a direct-ascent ASAT test in low Earth orbit (LEO), creating over 3,000 pieces of debris while demonstrating this key kinetic capability against space assets. One year later, the United States demonstrated a similar capability by destroying a malfunctioning satellite with an SM-3 missile. In 2020 alone, Russia conducted three ASAT tests, and India has now become the fourth country to demonstrate a successful test of a direct ascent ASAT missile. According to a recent report from the Center for Strategic and International Studies (CSIS), China's PLASSF has begun training specialized units for use of direct-ascent ASAT weapons capable of targeting assets in LEO.[10] CSIS further reports that China has demonstrated some of the technical capabilities required for a co-orbital ASAT capability. Additional counterspace capabilities are being tested and developed by space-faring nations, and Beijing has developed a range of other kinetic and nonkinetic counterspace technologies, such as directed-energy weapons, satellite jammers, and on-orbit satellites capable of proximity operations that could be leveraged in space operations.[11] Both the United States and China have tested proximity maneuvers in space and are developing ground-based lasers and jammers with the objective of

---

[8] Pollpeter, Chase, and Heginbotham, 2017; see also Costello and McReynolds, 2018.

[9] George, 2019.

[10] Harrison et al., 2020.

[11] For a comprehensive overview of Chinese space and counterspace capabilities, see Stokes et al., 2020.

interfering with satellite performance.[12] The testing of counterspace capabilities highlights a growing challenge for protecting space assets in the future.

Washington's reliance on space-based capabilities to support terrestrial operations, coupled with the increasing development of counterspace capabilities around the globe, has prompted growing interest in seeking deterrence in the space domain. The U.S. 2020 *Defense Space Strategy Summary* states that "ensuring the availability of these capabilities is fundamental to establishing and maintaining military superiority across all domains and to advancing U.S. and global security and economic prosperity."[13] However, there are multiple views on what is meant by "space deterrence," and it is important to bound the challenge before we address it. The most straightforward definition of space deterrence is the persuasion of an adversary to not "disrupt, deny, degrade, or destroy the space assets on which a nation relies."[14] Space assets, according to this definition, include systems that are in the space domain *and* systems that are supporting the space domain from the ground. For the purpose of this research report, we define *space deterrence* as the deterrence of interference with any systems that operate in space or support the operation of space systems from the ground.[15] This interference could take the form of actions against space assets themselves, ranging from dazzling a satellite's optics or jamming downlinks to the use of kinetic weapons against these satellites, or it could take the form of actions against ground-based assets that support space-based capabilities. Because space capabilities are

---

[12] In 2010, China launched the SJ-12 satellite and conducted a series of remote proximity maneuvers with an older Chinese satellite (Harrison et al., 2020). In 2003, the United States Air Force (USAF) launched the XSS-10 on a Delta-2 rocket and conducted a series of rendezvous and proximity operations maneuvers near the Delta upper stage (Pfrang, Kaila, and Weeden, 2020).

[13] DoD, 2020a, p. 1.

[14] Finch and Steene, 2011, p. 12.

[15] An important distinction here is that "space deterrence" is a means of deterring attacks *against* satellites and related space systems. Space capabilities can also be used for the *purpose* of deterrence. The latter is discussed further in Chapter Four when we consider China's approach to deterrence.

also a supporting infrastructure for terrestrial operations, achieving space deterrence requires a discussion that extends beyond the boundaries of the space domain. In this report, following a discussion of some key components of classical deterrence theory, we will explore further how space deterrence encompasses other domains and how space deterrence can be tailored to deter aggression and interference from China in this domain.

Since the purpose of this report is to consider potential ways in which the United States, along with key allies and partners, can effectively deter China in space, we systematically examined classical deterrence literature, recently published commentaries and academic papers on deterrence strategy in the space domain, and a broad set of primary source documents representing China's objectives and strategy in space. We first looked at classical deterrence literature to provide a structured background of key tenets for any deterrence strategy. Since much of this literature is based on nuclear deterrence during the Cold War, we then researched in this same literature how the context of nuclear deterrence specifically shaped the development of deterrence strategy. To help build an explanation for how space deterrence might be different, we then looked at current publications from researchers on security cooperation in space to identify characteristics of the space domain and how they differ from the nuclear context. Having identified key features of a space deterrence strategy more generally, we then look to build an approach for a deterrence strategy in this domain tailored to China. We used primary source documents to examine Beijing's goals and its own approach to deterrence in the space domain and examined how these particular goals may challenge some elements of an effective deterrence strategy in space. Using these key findings from the literature, we then assess potential implications for the United States, allies, and partners in the Indo-Pacific.

CHAPTER TWO

Key Features of Classical Deterrence Theory

The start of the Cold War and the implications of nuclear weapons brought deterrence to the forefront of national security strategy. Much of the development of classical deterrence theory therefore took place in an era of binary great-power competition and mutually assured destruction.[1] Alexander George and Richard Smoke define deterrence as "the persuasion of one's opponent that the costs and/or risks of a given course of action he might take outweigh its benefits."[2] The general objective of this deterrence is to "reduce the probability of enemy military moves inimical to one's self."[3] To achieve this objective, William Kaufmann describes a successful deterrence strategy as one in which there is both an expressed intention and demonstrated capability to defend or inflict cost on a prospective attacker, such that that attacker would not perceive the attack as worthwhile.[4] At the heart of this concept is the idea that deterrence should *convince* an adversary not to engage in a behavior because to do so would result

---

[1]   As the strategic implications of nuclear weapons were considered, the power of these weapons was not in their deployment but in the power of their threat. As Brodie, 1946, p. 7, points out, "Thus far the chief purpose of our military establishment has been to win wars. From now on, its chief purpose must be to avert them." This shift from winning wars brought deterrence to a prominent role in overall security strategy. For an overview of the role of RAND deterrence research over the past six decades, see Long, 2008.

[2]   George and Smoke, 1974, p. 11.

[3]   Objective of deterrence as stated in Snyder, 1960, p. 167.

[4]   See Kaufmann, 1972.

in *unacceptable losses*. Further, Thomas Schelling, among others, adds that for a threat to be an effective deterrent, it must be clearly communicated and the outcome demanded be plainly specified.[5] The essence of good deterrence, therefore, is not actually imposing costs or denying gains, but rather persuading the adversary of your ability and intent to do so. How this is accomplished as part of a deterrence strategy will depend on the nature of the conflict and the characteristics of the adversary.

Offense Dominance and Deterrence via Punishment

In classical deterrence theory, costs and risks can be imposed on an adversary via denial of gains or via punishment; either way, the intent is to convince an adversary that the cost of taking a specific action would outweigh the gains of taking that action. Deterrence by *denial* requires various defensive capabilities, the credibility of which depend on their perceived level of resilience, including redundancy and reconstitution capabilities, and effectiveness, which in turn may often be ascertained by the relative military power of the actors in conflict.[6] Deterrence by *punishment* requires the ability to retaliate following an attack. Here, *if* an actor retains the ability to respond following an attack (i.e., the strike did not eliminate their ability to deploy a nuclear weapon), the credibility of this approach often relies not on the relative military power of the actors but instead on the *intent* of the actor responding.[7]

During the 1950s, the threat of nuclear weapons created an environment of offense dominance. *Offense dominance* refers to a scenario in which a conflict is heavily weighted in favor of the offensive actions because defenses are largely ineffective against a determined offense. Because of this offense dominance, both the United States and the Soviet

---

[5] See, for example, Schelling, 1960; George and Smoke, 1974.

[6] For a further discussion of deterrence by denial, see Snyder, 1959.

[7] Snyder, 1959.

Union focused on deterrence by punishment, each growing its own nuclear arsenals to ensure the ability to retaliate. As secretary of defense in the Kennedy administration, Robert McNamara posited that avoiding escalation and a nuclear arms race relied on the mutual capability of the United States and Soviet Union to destroy each other, rather than on the ability of each party to defend against an attack.[8] In this manner, assured retaliation provided deterrence via threat of punishment.

Assured Retaliation, Credibility, and Attribution

The ability to retaliate is itself not sufficient to deter an adversary. This ability and the intent to use it must be clearly and credibly communicated.[9] Credible assured retaliation during the Cold War relied on full transparency about the deterrer's second-strike capabilities—that is, its nuclear arsenal's ability to survive a nuclear attack and launch a retaliatory strike. Similarly, for credible assured retaliation to be an effective component of a deterrence strategy in space, a potential aggressor should have no doubt about the deterrer's ability to retaliate and its intention to do so.

A vital enabler of assured retaliation is the ability to recognize and attribute an attack, so that you know against whom you must retaliate. Without the ability to attribute attacks, response options are constrained and likely escalatory. During the Cold War, the ability of the United States to recognize the nature and source of an attack meant that attribution was not a barrier to deterrence. It was acknowledged that this attribution capability would validate an appropriate retaliatory threat. But if circumstances are such that an attack cannot be characterized or its source identified, then the threat of punitive retaliation has little deterrent value.

---

[8]   This idea is summarized in Mutschler, 2013. The summary presented there is based on discussion in Yanarella, 1977.

[9]   Western thinking on deterrence includes the concept of clear redlines, but also the idea that ambiguity could have a role to play in building effective deterrence. Schelling, 1996, proposes that "leaving something to chance" could enhance deterrence.

Mutual Vulnerability and First-Strike Stability

Assured retaliatory capability and mutual vulnerability together provide what is described by Schelling and Brodie as first-strike stability, a condition that arises when neither side sees an advantage to striking first. Each of them notes in their seminal works that instability occurs when one side perceives that, by striking first, it can destroy the other's capability to retaliate. First-strike *instability* therefore occurs when one side perceives an advantage to striking first to avoid a worse outcome that would occur should it wait and incur a first strike itself.[10] If the potential aggressor does not have the ability (or would have a significantly degraded ability) to retaliate following a devastating strike, it may have an incentive to preempt out of fear that it will not get an opportunity to strike otherwise in what amounts to a "use-it-or-lose-it" scenario. Therefore, the ability of both sides to retaliate promotes first-strike stability.[11] According to Wohlstetter, terror and fear are also critical parts of deterrence strategy, because the principle of assured retaliation rests on the belief that fear of punishment shapes an adversary's risk calculus. Kahn adds that "frightening" is even a desirable attribute of deterrence.[12] First-strike stability, is therefore enhanced by the communication of credible and fear-inducing retaliatory capabilities.

The deterrent relationship between the United States and the Soviet Union during the Cold War was premised on each side's possessing the ability to inflict unacceptable costs on the other in a nuclear exchange. This concept, known as mutual assured destruction, relies on the vulnerability to a nuclear strike and the ability to retaliate should one occur. This mutual vulnerability between the two actors helped shape behavior and limitations on nuclear weapons and their delivery systems, including the Anti-Ballistic Missile Treaty, which limited the number of land-based antiballistic missile systems and prohibited the

---

[10] For further discussion of first-strike stability, see Mueller et al., 2006. See also Kent and Thaler, 1989.

[11] For description of crisis stability and a further discussion of first strike stability, see, for example, Kent and Thaler, 1989; Glaser, 1990; Sigal, 1985.

[12] Wohlstetter, 1958; Kahn, 1961.

development, testing, and deployment of air-, sea-, space-, and mobile land-based antiballistic missile systems capable of countering attacks by nuclear-armed strategic ballistic missiles.

Deterrence relied not only on the ability of both sides to inflict unacceptable costs, but also on the vulnerability of both sides to such retaliation in a way that highlights how these concepts coexisted in deterrence strategies in this era. The loss of mutual vulnerability between two actors can be destabilizing. This situation is one manifestation of a "security dilemma," wherein one actor's enhancement of its own security makes the other actor feel more vulnerable, and therefore more likely to take preventive or preemptive offensive action.[13] Embedded in the concept of first-strike stability, therefore, is a symmetric ability to incur and impose costs.

The perceptions of vulnerability and costs of action are vital to shaping any deterrence strategy. It is these perceptions that are the levers for shaping adversary behavior, and these concepts as perceived by China in the context of the space domain will be the key to an effective tailored deterrence strategy. The above discussion has identified some key elements of classical deterrence theory—namely, the importance of perceived costs and gains from an attack and how the perception of incurred cost relies on credible retaliation and mutual vulnerability. The following chapter examines the relevance of these key elements to deterrence in the space domain to inform how a deterrence strategy should be tailored to this domain.

---

[13] This concept of a security dilemma is discussed in further detail in Jervis, 1976, and Herz, 1950.

CHAPTER THREE

Tailoring Deterrence for the Space Domain

Classical deterrence theory outlines the need for managing perceptions of vulnerability, building a credible and assured means of denying gains or inflicting punishment, and clearly communicating this threat and the intent to carry it out. Deterrence strategy in the context of the space domain can be expected to involve these same efforts, though the approach for doing so may shift considerably due to the nature of what is being deterred. Space deterrence strategy requires a consideration of the characteristics of that domain and the nature of a conflict scenario that includes that domain. Further, and perhaps most importantly, a successful approach to deterrence in space requires an examination of what it means to shift from the deterrence *of a capability* to deterrence *in a domain*.

Cold War Deterrence Versus Deterrence in the Space Domain

While the destructive power of nuclear weapons prompted the emergence of deterrence theory as a significant part of national security strategy during the Cold War, the growing consideration of space deterrence is prompted by an increasing reliance on space for the military, civilian, and commercial capabilities it affords. The key objectives for nuclear deterrence were to prevent even limited use of nuclear weapons and, if deterrence failed, to preclude a conflict from escalating to total war. It was apparent that the stakes were high, with both parties in the bilateral competition recognizing that a nuclear conflict would be "total and ultimate, with the future of the world at stake."[1] The objective for space deterrence is to preserve the capabilities of space systems; though the impact of losing space-based capabilities range in severity, their loss is generally not perceived as "total and ultimate." In rethinking deterrence in the context of space, we consider that both the nature of what is being deterred and the nature of the stakes if deterrence fails are fundamentally different.

When we think about space deterrence today, we are no longer discussing how to deter the use of a specific capability, but instead how to deter the use of a variety of capabilities *in a specific domain*.[2] Space deterrence is therefore defined by the nature of the target, not the nature of the weapon.[3] While the specific objective of space deterrence as discussed in this research report is to prevent attacks in this domain, it is important to recognize the role of space deterrence as part of a larger deterrence strategy for protecting national security more generally. As pointed out by Marquez, the prevention of attacks against satellites and their supporting infrastructure is one of many interests in a broader strategy.[4] Further, some analysts assert that stable deterrence in space should be considered in the context of the broader deterrence

---

[1]   Morgan, 2003, p. 9.

[2]   The role of space systems has expanded, which, while not explicitly discussed here, is still a factor in how we think about the changing nature of deterrence in space. Deterrence during the Cold War then was closely linked to the safety of space assets because of their integration with nuclear force structures. It was presumed that an attack on space assets would necessarily be a prelude to or part of a nuclear confrontation, and because of this integration of space assets and strategic infrastructure, space deterrence was not then considered independently from the concepts of nuclear stability and deterrence.

[3]   This perspective follows the distinction made by Mueller, 2013, p. 45, who states that "the reason for framing nuclear deterrence as deterrence of nuclear use rather than deterrence by nuclear threat is that when we talk about space deterrence we almost always have in mind deterring attacks against satellites and related space systems, not the use of space capabilities for deterrent purposes, which is a vast and multifaceted subject given the variety of functions that space systems perform." These ideas are also discussed in Morgan, 2010.

[4]   Marquez, 2011.

relationship between two adversaries.[5] While space, in its supporting role for terrestrial conflict, may be an exceptionally attractive target for adversaries, the military balance of power and forces across *all* domains will determine whether deterrence in the space domain can be achieved. In this manner, space deterrence is not bound by weapon type or constrained to activity in the space domain. Because of this change in the context of what is being deterred, the strategy for achieving deterrence in space will most certainly necessitate a shift from nuclear deterrence in the Cold War.

Assured Retaliation and Multidomain Responses

This shift from deterring the use of a *capability* to deterring a type of *behavior* in a domain requires a shift in how the United States think about retaliation and response options. The United States currently enjoys an asymmetric advantage in military capabilities from space, and as a result, disruption of these capabilities will have a greater impact on the United States.[6] A retaliation from the United States against an aggressor's own space assets will have a lower impact if the aggressor does not share a symmetric level of reliance on these assets. This makes space systems an attractive target for an adversary if retaliatory actions are confined to the space domain. However, an attack on a space asset will not necessarily incite a retaliatory response *in the space domain*. The December 2020 National Space Policy states that "any purposeful interference with or an attack upon the space systems of the United States or its allies that directly affects national rights will be met with a deliberate response at a time, place, manner, and domain of our choosing."[7] Because the United States may choose to respond to attacks against space assets in a different domain, deterring action *in* the space domain will require a broader accounting of military

---

5 Finch and Steene, 2011.

6 Astorino-Courtois, 2017.

7 U.S. Office of Space Commerce, 2020.

capabilities as part of a larger deterrence strategy from a multidomain perspective. Even if United States space assets are an attractive target for an adversary, the threat and ability of the United States to retaliate anywhere, in any domain, could make the costs to an adversary of attacking space assets unacceptable, depending on the *balance of power across domains* and the *credibility of a response in another domain.* Responses to an attack in one domain that result in effects in another domain can be referred to as "cross-domain."[8] Assessing the effectiveness of these response types in a deterrence strategy requires an understanding of how an adversary perceives this threat and the challenge of shaping this perception. As Schelling points out, a threat is more credible to an adversary if it is perceived as "in the same currency, to respond in the same language, to make the punishment fit the character of the crime."[9] Establishing deterrence using cross-domain effects may thus require a focus on establishing the credibility of these threats.[10]

The Challenge of Asymmetric Vulnerability

Strategy for nuclear deterrence was shaped by the devastating nature of the weapon and the shared vulnerability to this weapon. During the Cold War, there was an understanding that, in principle, nothing could be protected from a determined attacker and that both sides were vulnerable to such an attack, and this created the conditions for mutual vulnerability and offense dominance. While space deterrence is not defined by the assumption of mutual devastation should deterrence fail, the context of space is still perceived by many as one in which all space systems to some extent have a shared vulnerability due to the challenge of developing comprehensive defenses for these systems, which, in turn, can potentially create an environment of offense

---

[8]   See discussion in Manzo, 2011.

[9]   Schelling, 1966, p. 146.

[10]   Cross-domain effects need not be limited to military domains and can include effects in diplomatic, information, military, and economic dimensions.

dominance in space.[11] Though the vulnerability of assets in the space domain is shared, the reliance on assets in the space domain is not. Since the dependence on the domain itself is asymmetric, the impact of an attack will necessarily be felt more acutely by actors with a greater presence in that domain. Without mutual and symmetric dependency, targeting assets in space that support actors with a high level of dependency, such as the United States, becomes much more appealing. For this reason, an adversary may be motivated to target any perceived vulnerability, and the willingness of an adversary to exploit this asymmetric vulnerability *may depend on its own presence in the space domain and the perception of the level of this asymmetry.* Further, while in the Cold War shared vulnerability contributed to shaping behavior and constraining the development of nuclear weapons and their delivery systems, asymmetry in this vulnerability in the space domain may be a barrier to similar developments in establishing behavioral norms and treaties. Actors with less at stake in the space domain are less compelled to sign on to or abide by behavioral norms that would constrain their actions.

Capability and Credibility of Attribution

A successful deterrence strategy requires the ability to detect and attribute an action to the aggressor. However, detection and attribution in space are recognized as significant technological challenges. For example, the effects of debris or natural phenomena such as geomagnetic storms can interfere with satellite operations, making it difficult to

---

[11] While it is frequently recognized that space systems are characterized by some level of vulnerability, the idea that space is inherently offense-dominant is not a universally accepted one. One argument is that this idea of space as offense-dominant is premised on a consideration of individual satellites and their vulnerability, but if we look at the end use of these satellites and how measures such as proliferation could complicate an adversary's ability to attack, this shifts the offense-defense balance. See, for example, Townsend, 2020. In recognition that it is often easier to attack than defend, we adopt the designation from Van Evera, 1998, and use the phrase "offense dominant" to mean that offense is "easier than usual" but not necessarily easier than defense.

determine whether interference might be due to an intentional attack.[12] Recognizing the important role of attribution as a cornerstone of any deterrence strategy, the United States needs to continue to develop *and demonstrate* an ability to attribute attacks on its space systems in order to establish credible and assured retaliation.[13] The importance of developing these capabilities is reflected in the increasing prioritization of space domain awareness (SDA) in the USSF and United States Space Command.[14] Some level of adversary awareness of these SDA capabilities is required for them to act as a deterrent, and for this reason their development needs to be accompanied by a focus on strategic messaging and communication.

If the United States would like to deter attacks and other forms of threatening behavior, imposing costs outside of the military domain could be considered. The threat of retaliation outside of strictly military measures requires a consideration of global perceptions as well as those of an adversary. For example, if a threatened retaliatory response includes the imposition of a political cost, then the effectiveness of this threat not only relies on the *ability* to attribute, but also on the *perception* of this ability in the larger global community. To impose a political cost, there must be a perception among global stakeholders that the aggressor has indeed done something that violates norms or other behavioral guidelines. For this political cost to factor into adversary decisionmaking, the level of attribution must be sufficient to convince these key audiences. However, as noted by General Shelton in 2017, anonymity as an aggressor is easier to achieve in space.[15] Identifying the source of nonkinetic attacks in space can be particularly difficult.

---

[12] The challenge of attribution is further complicated by increasing dual-use assets in space and the resulting entanglement and potential blurring of intent.

[13] For further discussion, see Gleason and Hays, 2020.

[14] Erwin, 2020. USAF Space Command recently shifted its terminology from the use of space situational awareness describing catalog maintenance to the use of SDA to include the detection and characterization of all threat types (Erwin, 2019). Recent comments from Maj. Gen. Leah Lauderback, USSF director of intelligence, surveillance, and reconnaissance state that the ability to characterize threats and distinguish them from benign objects is a major challenge for the USSF (Erwin, 2021a).

[15] See Shelton, 2017.

If the United States would like to deter threatening behavior short of attacks, the challenge of doing so is compounded by the difficulty of distinguishing between offensive and defensive weapons in space, which thus leaves open the possibility of claims from an aggressor that an observed threatening behavior was in fact benign.[16] For an adversary to incur a political cost for its behavior, there needs to be a valid claim that it has done something wrong. If offensive and defensive capabilities can be perceived as somewhat indistinguishable, it is harder to create the perception that any posturing with this capability is threatening behavior in violation of accepted behavioral guidelines of norms.

When actions by potential adversaries are not readily observable or attributable, an adversary seeking to avoid punishment that relies on this attribution is less easily deterred. A successful strategy for space deterrence therefore *requires addressing this challenge of attribution* through improved SDA and strategic messaging to the global community that includes clear behavioral guidelines.

Establishing Behavioral Norms in Space

Space has only recently emerged as a domain of conflict, and clear guidelines for acceptable behavior in space have not yet been established. There is a legal prohibition against the use of some space weapons, as enshrined in the 1967 Outer Space Treaty, which prohibits both the placement of weapons of mass destruction in orbit and on any celestial body and the use of celestial bodies for military bases, testing, or maneuvers.[17] The treaty does not, however, make clear what is meant by "weapons of mass destruction," nor does it prohibit launching weapons *through* space. While emphasizing the peaceful use of space, this treaty is seen by many as inadequate guidance to address militarization in this domain, and many states have been calling for the adop-

---

[16] While the stability of deterrence or likelihood of deterrence failure is not explicitly discussed in this report, it is notable that the combination of offense dominance and the inability to distinguish between offensive and defensive capabilities could be exceptionally destabilizing. This situation is dubbed "doubly dangerous" by Jervis, 1978.

[17] For the status of UN agreements related to outer space, see United Nations Office for Outer Space Affairs, 2021.

tion of a treaty specifically on the prevention of an arms race in space. Several countries, including China and Russia, are currently pursuing multilateral negotiations against the weaponization of space. However, the Russian and Chinese draft treaty on Prohibition of Placement of Weapons in Outer Space and the Threat or Use of Force against Space Objects introduced in the United Nations Conference on Disarmament under the Prevention of an Arms Race in Outer Space agenda, would only prohibit the placement of weapons in outer space. It does not address terrestrial threats to space systems.

Explicit behavioral guidelines among all global stakeholders could help to support stability in the space domain, and reliance on tacit agreements may produce an environment that is more difficult to stabilize. Further, Schelling points out that, while tacit agreements are possible, they do not always succeed, and even if they do "there is no assurance that . . . it will yield to either party a particularly favorable outcome compared with alternatives that might have been available if full communication had been allowed."[18] Explicit guidance on what is unacceptable in the space domain may be an important tool for persuading an adversary that constraining its behavior is a better outcome than breaching these established guidelines.

In the absence of widely accepted behavioral norms, overt signaling to specific adversaries of clear redlines and acceptable behavior in the space domain may similarly impact adversary decision calculus. For this approach, the deterrer needs to provide clear signals tailored to the potential aggressor about which acts it perceives to be unacceptable.[19] These signals, though targeted to a specific adversary, need to be communicated to the global community at large if potential political costs of violating these norms is part of the deterrence strategy. If the United States would like to shape a potential adversary's decision cal-

---

[18] Schelling, 1960, p. 77.

[19] "China's tactic for many years has been to blur the red lines that might otherwise lead to open confrontation with the United States too early for Beijing's liking. The United States must be very clear about which Chinese actions it will seek to deter and, should deterrence fail, will prompt direct American intervention. These should be unambiguously communicated to Beijing through high-level diplomatic channels so that China is placed on notice." See "To Counter China's Rise, the U.S. Should Focus on Ji," 2021.

culus regarding aggressive action in space using political costs, it needs to articulate *publicly* what it considers to be unacceptable behavior by an adversary in space.[20] Further, the global audience of this messaging needs to buy in to these guidelines of acceptable behavior, and communication of these behavioral guidelines needs to be coupled with the credibility of the *intent* to retaliate if necessary. Effectively threatening a political cost then requires not only effective public messaging and acceptance from the global recipients of this messaging, but also the perception of the adversary that the threat of political retaliation is credible based on whether it believes the message and whether it believes that the United States would indeed follow through on this threat.[21] An adversary that is made aware of the threat of retaliation will likely consider any past demonstration of willingness to follow through in its decision calculus. Deterrence in space therefore may benefit from previous demonstrations of a willingness to respond in other domains.[22]

Establishing behavioral guidelines and redlines can take a variety of forms, including the communication of well-defined technical boundaries or messaging that helps establish boundaries for unacceptable behavior in space. Here we see another important departure from the nuclear deterrence that results from the shift from deterrence of a capability to deterrence in a domain. When deterring the use of a capability, such as nuclear weapons, what defines this weapon and its use has a clear technical definition. When deterring in the space domain, these technical definitions may not be as clear. Actors in the space domain do not necessarily agree on what constitutes threatening behavior, and ambiguous capabilities make any violation of redlines and

---

[20] This strategy relies on the adversary valuation of political capital. Rogue actors are less concerned with their political standing. Understanding how an adversary weighs political capital relative to military objectives is important for determining whether this strategy for cost imposition could be a successful one.

[21] A detailed discussion of the role of trust in international relations can be found in Kydd, 2005.

[22] Schelling, 1966, p. 36, states that "to fight abroad is a military act, but to persuade enemies or allies that one would fight abroad, under circumstances of great cost and risk, requires more than a military capability. It requires having those intentions . . . and communicating them persuasively to make other countries behave."

behavioral guidelines more challenging to establish. Further, while technical definitions of unacceptable or threatening behavior could be made clear and specific, such as a specified range of exclusion zones for satellite proximity, this may invite an adversary to approach these boundaries without actually breaching them, and continuing techno-logical advances could require these redlines to frequently shift. In the space domain, technical redlines are more difficult to establish, and even if they were, such technical thresholds may be unstable as tech-nologies advance. More robust redlines may rely instead on defining behaviors, not capabilities, that are unacceptable. While unambigu-ous *technical* redlines may encourage gray-zone tactics, unambiguous *behavioral* redlines may promote deterrence.[23] For example, the United States has provided a message defining unacceptable behavior in space as "any purposeful interference with or an attack upon critical com-ponents of our space architecture that directly affects this vital United States interest."[24] This message targets behaviors and avoids technical redlines. This message is also ambiguous enough to leave room for adversaries to interpret what is meant by "interference," and in doing so discourages adversaries who may otherwise seek to operate in the gray zone just shy of a more specific threshold.[25]

Communication of Capabilities and Intent

This message from the United States defining unacceptable behav-ior is itself not enough to deter. While establishing clear behavioral guidelines is an important element of a space deterrence strategy, these

---

[23] Marquez, 2011, p. 16, notes that "setting redlines that are focused on the capabilities of certain weapons invites an adversary to approach but not cross a redline."

[24] U.S. Office of Space Commerce, 2020.

[25] Here is another instance in which an understanding of the adversary has significant importance. Adversaries may be motivated to violate ambiguous redlines by finding room for interpretation to the contrary. On the other hand, adversaries may be deterred from violating ambiguous redlines because of the increased risk of accidental crossing of this redline. Under-standing the adversary's propensity for operating in the gray zone as well as their perception of the role of uncertainty in a deterrence strategy is important for shaping strategy here.

guidelines may not be effective if there is not also a clearly communicated *ability* and *intent* to hold violators accountable. The *ability* to hold violators accountable relies on attribution, and the United States has developed its own messaging to assert its ability to detect and attribute. For example, in discussing the declassification of the Geosynchronous Space Situational Awareness Program, General Hyten asserted that the goal of this declassification was to "send a message to the world that says: Anything you do in the geosynchronous orbit we will know about. Anything."[26] However, communicating the *intent* to impose a suitable cost on violators may be more challenging, and this challenge is compounded by the lack of behavioral guidelines that clearly indicate unacceptable behavior.

The absence of acceptable behavioral guidelines, coupled with a lack of clear intent to punish violators, will significantly degrade the efficacy of deterrence, as exhibited by recent activity by Russia and the response from the United States. In a series of public statements from the United States Space Command in response to Russian ASAT testing, the United States attempted to establish that Russia is in violation of behavioral norms in space. This messaging focused on communicating behavioral guidelines and establishing this Russian activity as a violation of these guidelines. In July 2020, the United States Space Command alleged that "Russia conducted a non-destructive test of a space-based anti-satellite weapon."[27] In response to this test, Christopher Ford, U.S. undersecretary for arms control and international security, said that the test "highlights Russia's hypocritical advocacy of outer space arms control, with which Moscow aims to restrict the capabilities of the United States while clearly having no intention of halting its own counterspace program." Following a December 2020 ASAT test, the third that year, the United States Space Command stated that "Russia publicly claims it is working to prevent the transformation of outer space into a battlefield, yet at the same time Moscow continues to weaponize space by developing and fielding on-orbit and ground-based capabilities that seek to exploit U.S. reliance on

---

[26] Statement from General Hyten, quoted in Gruss, 2015.

[27] U.S. Space Command Public Affairs Office, 2020a.

space-based systems."[28] These statements sought to indicate that Russia violated even its own behavioral norms in space. However, the statement to this effect following the first ASAT test appears to have been ineffective at deterring the following two.

The strength of these statements from the United States relies on whether there is a credible threat of paying punitive costs should Russia continue to conduct these tests. The fact that there were three such tests last year may indicate that this threat is not credible and highlight that establishing this credibility should be an important focus of a future messaging strategy. To enhance the efficacy of its messaging, the United States could tailor its declaratory policy—and actions such as doctrine, training, and exercises—in visible ways that would *enhance the credibility of the intent* to retaliate and thereby have greater impact on the adversary's *perceptions of political and military cost* of aggressive actions in space.

Elements of a Deterrence Strategy for Space

From this discussion, it is apparent that constructing a deterrence strategy for the space domain requires addressing some specific challenges due to the characteristics of this domain and the context of who and what is to be deterred. The asymmetry of reliance on space-based capabilities, the possibility of cross-domain responses, and the difficulty of establishing credible attribution all contribute challenges to the building of a deterrence strategy for space. A deterrence strategy for space therefore needs to build credibility and legitimacy of cross-domain responses, account for asymmetric vulnerabilities, and communicate attribution capabilities and intent. Messaging and norms are an important tool for a deterrence strategy in space, but the success of this approach relies heavily on the target of these messages. For this reason tailoring a deterrence strategy to a particular adversary is especially important, and the next chapter will examine how China's objectives, perceptions, and behavior in the space domain set the context for tailoring a deterrence strategy targeted toward this particular actor.

---

[28] U.S. Space Command Public Affairs Office, 2020b.

CHAPTER FOUR

Tailoring Deterrence for China

Because of China's expressed ambitions and objectives in space—namely, preventing United States hegemony there and more globally—deterring China from interfering with space-based capabilities is of particular interest to the United States and its allies. Achieving deterrence in the space domain against China requires a specific consideration of how Chinese political decisionmakers assess the credibility of threats to retaliate, how they perceive potential punitive costs should they choose to attack, and, importantly, how such an attack might support their objectives despite the costs. This chapter thus examines China's objectives in the space domain as stated in primary source documents to help build an understanding of its perception of cost and benefit from actions in space. Imposing a high cost on China for aggressive action in space also requires understanding both its perceptions of the credibility of retaliation and its calculation of military and political costs of the action being considered.[1] Considering objectives and perceptions from a Chinese perspective will help to identify an effective approach for building a tailored deterrence strategy.

---

[1]   This section is meant to provide a brief illustration of the concepts discussed in this report in the context of a tailored deterrence strategy for China in space. For a more in-depth discussion of tailored deterrence as a concept, see Nakatani, forthcoming.

People's Liberation Army Space Objectives and Approach to Space Deterrence

China has an ambitious set of objectives in space. It seeks to become a "space giant" to bolster overall Chinese strength while also recognizing space as a key enabler in a terrestrial conflict.[2] China views U.S. activity in space as an obstacle to these goals. Accordingly, to achieve its objectives in space, China is seeking to offset any military, commercial, or civilian advantages to the United States from space-based capabilities and views these space-based capabilities, including reconnaissance, early warning, communication, and navigation systems, as attractive targets for an attack.[3] China perceives space as a critical United States vulnerability and has counterspace weapons capable of targeting nearly every class of United States space assets.[4] These military objectives indicate both the importance and the difficulty of deterring China in this domain.

Chinese military objectives in space are apparent from both official and semiofficial primary source publications. At the most authoritative level, President Xi during his 19th Party Congress speech in October 2017 emphasized the importance of China eventually becoming a nation of innovators across all domains, including in "aerospace."[5] Doing so would help Xi eventually achieve his "China

---

[2] In June 2013, Xi Jinping made a statement during a video call with the astronauts on the Shenzhou X mission about China pursuing a "space dream" as part of an overall effort to bolster Chinese strength (Xin, 2013). In 2016, China stated a goal of becoming a "space giant" ("Make China a Global Space Giant: Xi Jinping," 2016). Further, the Chinese strategic community recognizes space as a key enabler in a terrestrial conflict. See Vasani, 2017.

[3] Ashley, 2019.

[4] U.S.-China Economic and Security Review Commission, 2019. China has long been developing and testing means of denying image collections from overhead U.S. satellites, and one focus has been the development of ground-based directed energy weapons for laser dazzling of optical equipment on satellites. Gen. Raymond, the commander of SPACECOM and the USAF Space Command, has asserted that China is developing laser weapons with the intent of blinding U.S. satellites (Mayfield, 2019). An assessment from January 2019 warned that China is likely to field a ground-based laser weapon that can counter low-orbit sensors in 2020 (U.S. Defense Intelligence Agency, 2019).

[5] Xi, 2017.

Dream" of national rejuvenation. Indeed, while talking to Chinese astronauts in 2013, Xi described his "space dream" as part of his overall China Dream, noting that China would become stronger "with the development of space programs."[6] Beijing's focus on space resulted in the publication of the "White Paper on China's Space Activities in 2016," which stated that its goal is "to build China into a space power in all respects . . . [in part] to effectively and reliably guarantee national security."[7] China's latest defense white paper, published in 2019, highlights the need "to safeguard China's security interests in outer space." It further states that Beijing's ultimate goal is "to safely enter, exit, and openly use outer space"—movements Chinese leaders do not believe are guaranteed as space increasingly becomes "a critical domain in international strategic competition."[8] Notably, and in line with Beijing's consistent and public position to leverage space exclusively for peaceful and scientific purposes, neither Xi nor any other authority directly addresses Chinese military ambitions and preparations in space.

Nevertheless, it is clear from semiofficial publications, particularly PLA writings, that Beijing has big plans for space. According to a Western analysis of Chinese military writings, the overarching assumption among Chinese analysts is "the belief that 'whoever controls space controls the Earth.'" Pollpeter and colleagues further observe that "this belief is based on the premise that space is the new high ground on which success on the terrestrial battlefield is based. Indeed, space is so important to [PLA] battlefield success that conducting modern war is not possible without its effective use." They go on to note that Chinese military analysts believe they "must first seize the initiative in space . . . [which] will require China to achieve space supremacy, defined as the ability to freely use space and to deny the use of space to adversaries."[9] Another Western analysis of PLA writings, conducted by

---

[6] Xin, 2013.

[7] China National Space Administration, 2016, p. 2.

[8] State Council Information Office of the People's Republic of China, 2019, p. 13.

[9] Pollpeter et al., 2015, p. 8.

Dean Cheng, reveals that Beijing first fully understood the importance of space following the U.S. military's successful ability during the first Gulf War (1991) to leverage satellites in support of joint military operations against Iraq.[10] Since that time, China has been intensely focused on establishing information dominance over the United States to support future PLA warfighting, including the collection, dissemination, and protection of data using space-based assets. The idea is that information dominance in space will further enable a "system-of-systems" approach to PLA joint operations—that is, a fully integrated military network in which command and control decisions are optimized through real-time intelligence collection and analysis of the battlespace across all domains.[11] In pursuit of this key objective, China in late 2015 established the PLASSF, which is charged with carrying out the majority of PLA space activities and integrating all forms of information in support of space, cyber, and electromagnetic capabilities.[12]

Semiofficial Chinese military writings also offer valuable perspectives on deterrence in a broad sense, as well as on space deterrence. It is clear that China's definition of deterrence is not exactly congruent with the Western definition, even though Western concepts are taught in Chinese schools. Generally, the West defines deterrence as convincing an adversary—whether through denial, punishment, or both—that the risks or costs of certain actions are too high to proceed (*compellence*, a closely associated term, means to do this while adversary action is already underway in order to convince the adversary to stop).[13] The Chinese version of deterrence, however, goes further than the Western definition.[14] Known as *weishe*, this version adds psycho-

---

[10] Cheng, 2018.

[11] Engstrom, 2018.

[12] Pollpeter, Chase, and Heginbotham, 2017.

[13] For the seminal Western work on deterrence, see Schelling, 1966. See also George and Smoke, 1974, and Mazarr, 2018. For official government definitions of "deterrence" and "compellence," see Joint Chiefs of Staff, 2019, pp. II-4, II-5.

[14] For additional background on *weishe*, see U.S. National Academy of Sciences and Chinese People's Association for Peace and Disarmament, 2008.

logical pressure to the adversary's decisionmaking "to submit to the deterrer's volition."[15] In essence, this means that Beijing seeks not only to deter a single adversary action, but also to undermine the entirety of an adversary's plan to wage conflict against China. Thus, *weishe* is intended to have far greater impact across warfighting domains. Thus, for example, PLA actions in space should convince the U.S. military to back down *not only* in space, but in other domains as well. This more expansive view of deterrence also indicates a greater importance placed on power projection from the space domain from China.

Regarding space deterrence, or *kongjian weishe*, Chinese military writings are not particularly direct. However, one semiofficial piece, *Course of Study of Space Operations*, which is a textbook for the Academy of Military Sciences, addresses the issue head on. The authors, Jiang Lianju and Wang Liwen, argue,

> Space deterrence refers to the use of threatened or actual limited use of space force, backed up by powerful space forces, to shock and awe or curb the adversary's military operations against them. The objective of this operation style is to demonstrate the strength and resolve of one's own space operations by creating an appearance, through the combination of intimidation and fighting, and making a show of power, which causes misgivings, fear, and wavering in the enemy, and compels it to abandon its operational intent or control its operational scale, intensity, and operational measures, thereby attaining the objective of subduing the enemy without fighting or only fighting [a] small battle.[16]

Jiang and Wang further argue that there are three nonviolent and one violent means of deterring adversaries in or through space. Their work clearly demonstrates that China conceptualizes space deterrence as both using space to deter an adversary and deterring an adversary's

---

[15] The phrase "to submit to the deterrer's volition" appears in the Academy of Military Sciences, 2005, p. 215. Cheng, 2011, p. 92, also refers to the phrase.

[16] Jiang and Wang, 2013, p. 122.

interference with space-based assets. Details on these means, as translated and assessed by Dean Cheng, are as follows:

1. *Displays of space forces and weapons:* In peacetime, the PLA showcases the effectiveness of certain space capabilities through state-run media outlets. Displays may also involve inviting foreign government representatives, such as defense attaches, to observe space testing and demonstrations.

2. *Military space exercises:* During crisis escalation, Beijing demonstrates PLA readiness to use space capabilities if the adversary is unprepared to back down,

3. *Space force deployments:* As the crisis continues to escalate, the PLA could reposition and array its forces in certain advantageous locations to overmatch adversarial forces.

4. *"Space shock and awe strikes":* If all the previous nonviolent actions fail to achieve the desired end state, then the PLA is prepared to launch punitive strikes to send the message that China will resolutely defend itself in space and leverage space for terrestrial-based joint military operations against the adversary.[17]

According to Jiang and Wang, punitive strikes can take two forms: "soft" and "hard." Soft strikes are essentially reversible in nature—thus, for example, "dazzling" rather than "destroying"—and may include cyberhacks, jamming, and spoofing. Hard strikes, in contrast, are designed to be irreversibly destructive in nature and could involve ASAT or use of directed-energy weapons against United States satellites or other space assets.

Underlying Chinese views of space deterrence is the notion that deterring in space should have cross-cutting effects on the adversary's abilities and resolve to continue fighting in other domains, whether on land, at sea, in the air, or in cyberspace. Indeed, Beijing, like Washington, does not view deterrence in space as affecting the adversary exclusively in the space domain. Rather, space deterrence should have an impact on all facets of the adversary's plans and capabilities, not only

---

[17] Cheng, 2018, p. 25. For original Chinese source content, see Sun and Chang, 2003, p. 33.

in space, but elsewhere as well. Ultimately, China seeks to use space deterrence activities to deter an adversary from starting (or continuing, in the form of compellence) conflict against it.

Shaping People's Liberation Army Perceptions of Gains and Costs

The preceding examination of China's objectives in space illustrates the particular challenges in deterring China from interfering with space-based operations. Space superiority is an explicit goal for China, and it may perceive that degrading the United States' ability to project power from space as a stepping-stone to achieving that goal. Primary sources document the important role of space in China's overall goal of "national rejuvenation" and indicate that any measures to help achieve dominance in space are perceived to have a high value if successful. Specifically, China's focus on information dominance points toward a highly perceived benefit both from developing its own capabilities and from interfering with space assets that support the information capabilities of the United States. China's approach to deterrence suggests that it may view a limited use of force in space as an effective deterrent against adversary military action elsewhere, thereby increasing the perceived benefits of demonstrations against space-based capabilities. Further, the perceived dependence of the United States on space-based capabilities is a vulnerability that tempts exploitation. China perceives a high potential gain from specifically targeting any vulnerabilities in space-based capabilities due to their current asymmetric reliance on this domain.

For the United States to meet these challenges, space deterrence requires decreasing the perceived utility of interfering with space-based capabilities, mitigating the perception that limited use of space force will act as a deterrent, and addressing the view of U.S. vulnerability in space. Because China perceives a large potential benefit from aggressive action in space, deterrence requires a response costly enough to offset China's perceived gains from interfering with United States space operations or a significant decrease in the perceived gains toward achieving space dominance should they choose to act.

One approach for increasing China's perceived cost of aggressive action is to impose costs outside the boundaries of the space domain. For example, economic or diplomatic sanctions could be implemented. Indeed, we see from the above discussion that China's own view of deterrence in space extends beyond the space domain. However, the success of this approach relies on persuading the global space community that China's actions are unacceptable. The current lack of widely accepted behavioral norms will make this particularly challenging. China may claim its actions are benign and, in doing so, avoid incurring any diplomatic or economic sanctions in response. To impose political costs, the global space community will need to be persuaded that the retaliatory response, from the United States or elsewhere, *is* acceptable. Since China has publicly adopted the position that space should be used exclusively for peaceful and scientific purposes, it may seek to shape any response to its activity in space as illegitimate and counter to those purposes to avoid potential political costs. Such an approach is challenging for any actor, but may be especially challenging when deterring China, given the high value it places on any potential gains in space dominance.

Defining guidelines for unacceptable activity in space could provide another means for increasing China's perceived costs for aggressive action in space. If these guidelines were to be established and accepted by the larger global community, an adversary wishing to avoid paying a high political cost may be deterred from violating them. This approach, however, requires that the adversary places sufficient value on its own political capital and perceives that this capital is at risk should it act. As China builds its own partnerships in the space domain, it may care less about the political capital lost among international stakeholders outside of these partnerships. Further, China may seek to establish a legitimacy for its own actions in space by messaging that the United States has already violated the peaceful use of space. One primary source document asserts that the establishment of USSF is one such example of a violation of the international system of the peaceful use of space.[18] According to this

---

[18] Li, Yao, and Cui, 2019.

document, the establishment of USSF will intensify tensions in space and could trigger an arms race.[19] In this manner, China could be setting the stage for justifying its own actions in space to the global community and using its own messaging strategy to avoid paying the full cost of breaking any established behavioral guidelines. China could also engage in a messaging campaign that attempts to divide the United States from its allies by asserting that USSF is engaging in destabilizing activities that it has not disclosed to these allies. China may gain an advantage by shaping global perceptions of United States' ambitions in space in order to legitimize its own activity. In light of these challenges, an effective approach to deterring China may encourage China and its allies to have a stake in the international space community and buy in to any established norms. However, as China strengthens its own partnerships in the space domain, it gains the ability to influence the shaping of behavioral norms in space and may become less incentivized to seek to comply with the behavioral norms sought out by the United States and its allies.[20]

Another approach to shaping the perceived utility of interfering with U.S. space-based capabilities is by seeking to decrease the perceived gains from doing so. However, China's perception of U.S. objectives in space may make shaping the perceived gains from interfering with U.S. space-based capabilities more difficult. If China perceives that the United States is seeking military hegemony in space—meaning that the United States is seeking to maintain not just the ability to project power from space, but a military advantage over other actors in space—China is less likely to believe U.S. statements asserting that its

---

[19] Note the dilemma faced by USSF in creating the impression that it supports the peaceful use of outer space while also signaling resolve. Statements from USSF attempt to address that; for example, Gen. Raymond stated during an Air Force Association 2020 Air, Space, and Cyber Conference that "the United States doesn't want to engage in warfare in space but must be prepared for such a scenario" (Lopez, 2020).

[20] China's collaboration with Russia to build a scientific research station on the moon is an example of a growing alliance that may have significant influence in crafting international space policy (and potentially diminish the influence of the United States in doing so). See Kramer, 2021.

space systems are not intended to threaten other assets in space.[21] In this case, the objective value for China for interfering with the operation of these space systems is increased, which, in turn, makes deterrence of an attack against these systems more challenging. The United States could also pursue this denial of gains strategy by shaping China's perceptions of deterrence. If its objective is to deter by a limited use of space force, the United States should pursue a messaging strategy that a demonstration of force on the part of China, instead of acting as a deterrent, would be perceived as escalatory and prompt a response from the United States. Decreasing the relative vulnerability of U.S. space-based assets is another avenue for denial of gains. While a loss of space capabilities is likely, at least in the near term, to be more consequential to the United States than to China in most scenarios,[22] the United States can use advantages in other domains to address the vulnerability that comes with asymmetric dependence on space capabilities.

Much of the above measures for building an effective deterrence strategy rely on legitimizing responses outside of the space domain. As discussed above, this legitimacy requires a shared understanding of what constitutes an appropriate and proportional response to attacks in space. Without this shared understanding, deterrent threats may not be credible, and if deterrence fails, a response could be perceived as disproportionate or illegitimate by China and lead to inadvertent escalation. Further, China could exploit perceived illegitimacy of a U.S. response to avoid political costs of the initial attack. The absence of a shared understanding leaves the door open for a savvy adversary to exploit a potential misinterpretation to legitimize its own actions.[23] To create a credible threat of assured retaliation, the United States needs not only to make clear to China that it is willing to engage and respond in other domains, but also to set the expectation that these responses are perceived as legitimate by the larger international community.

---

[21] This U.S. pursuit of hegemony in space is noted in primary source documents, including Zhao and Wei, 2020.

[22] Morgan, 2010. This situation may be shifting as the PLA's dependence on space to support operations distant from the Chinese mainland is deepening.

[23] This point is discussed in Manzo, 2011.

Elements of a Tailored Deterrence Strategy for China in Space

We have discussed features of space deterrence more generally and provided perspective on China's strategic objectives for the space domain. From this discussion, we can identify features of a tailored deterrence strategy for China in space. Some of these features may apply more generally to *any* adversary in the space domain, while some features and challenges are specific to China.

A space deterrence strategy tailored specifically for China will consider the high value China places on space capabilities and information dominance. If China perceives aggressive action in space as a means to achieve those objectives, the perceived cost of these aggressive actions will need to be high if China is to be deterred. If China does not care about the perceptions of the international community, or if it does care, but not enough to offset the perceived gains of aggressive action in space, then deterrence will be particularly challenging. As China builds its own partnerships in the space domain, most notably with Russia, these relationships may diminish the perceived political cost of violating any established behavioral norms and guidelines. Imposing political costs on China will require strategic coordination between the United States and its allies.

A tailored deterrence strategy for China in space will also consider China's growing reliance on its own space-based capabilities. Whether China grows to parity in terms of space power projection and reliance on space-based capabilities will shape how deterrence in this domain should be tailored to China. This growing reliance may decrease the perceived relative vulnerability of the United States' own space-based capabilities as the two powers approach parity in their power projection from this domain. An effective deterrence strategy tailored to China specifically may benefit from encouraging and highlighting this shared reliance on space-based capabilities.

Other elements of a space deterrence strategy for China are less specific to the adversary and are features of space deterrence more generally. A credible ability to attribute is vital to ensuring that China perceives a political cost for interference with a space asset. For China to perceive that it would pay a political cost, China needs to be convinced not only that the United States has the capability and intent to respond but also that the United States can sufficiently attribute the source of this interference and has mechanisms to share this information with allies and partners. Without the demonstrated ability to attribute, China could leverage any uncertainty to deny responsibility or intent of a threatening action targeting a space asset. The global community also needs to be convinced of this credible ability to attribute if China is to incur political costs for its actions. Imposing a political cost on China requires *establishing among the relevant global actors* the illegitimacy of the action and a credible means of attribution, for example, via enhanced SDA, and strategic communication of this capability.

Another general element of a space deterrence strategy is the managing of perceived legitimacy of considered responses to aggressive action. In order for a threatened response to be an effective deterrent, China, or any adversary, must perceive a willingness on the part of the United States to leverage punitive measures in other domains, and the global space community must perceive the legitimacy of these responses. From this we see that perceptions of the global community *and* perceptions of China are important to tailoring a deterrence strategy for China in space.

CHAPTER FIVE

Implications for the United States

A deterrence strategy tailored to the space domain will need to consider capabilities, actions, and retaliatory responses in other domains and use this to shape China's perception of the costs and gains of interfering in space. From our analysis here, several initial observations on how the United States could best shape China's perception of cost and gains become apparent.

First, given that Beijing clearly believes that space deterrence is part and parcel of undermining the overall will and capabilities of an adversary to resist in armed conflict, Washington might need to rethink how it responds to the Chinese escalation ladder. For example, if Beijing escalates from *military space exercises* to *space force deployments*, as described by Jiang and Wang above, then Washington should seek to convey to Beijing that its space deterrence strategy is not working. This would entail the United States demonstrating resolve to fight on in the confrontation, and might require meeting Chinese space escalation with countervailing U.S. responses in the space domain, other domains, or both. Doing so would reinforce the message that Beijing is failing to achieve the desired end state. Communicating the United States' ability and intent to respond in other domains is important for this tailored deterrence strategy. From this perspective, it is concerning that official U.S. space strategy still generally conceptualizes American space deterrence efforts as confined to the space domain. According to the Pentagon's *Defense Space Strategy Summary*, published in June 2020, Washington seeks "to deter and defeat adversary hostile use of space" in order to "maintain space superiority" as well as "deter aggression in space" to "ensure space stability."[1] The strategy does not address how Washington would effectively prevent Chinese actions in space from undermining terrestrial-based U.S. joint military operations in all other domains. In the first USSF Chief of Space Operations' planning guidance of November 2020, however, the United States approaches doing so by stating that "we will support a position of strategic stability, United States advantage in space, and a space warfighting posture that deters aggression and ensures Joint and Coalition warfighters can employ forces in the time, place, manner, and domain of our choosing."[2] Further, the United States Space Command, while previously focused on providing capabilities that support other military operations, such as communication satellites and missile warning, has shifted to a new paradigm that recognizes that, should U.S. space capabilities be targeted, the United States Space Command would need to be supported by other combatant commands.[3] These recent shifts that recognize the supporting and supported role of the space domain are positive moves toward a multidomain approach to space deterrence. The bottom line is that the United States' public statements should avoid space-to-space calculations and encompass deterring China's plans to impact the entirety of the United States' war effort through activities in space. Doing so could convince Beijing that such a plan would not work, or at least that it would be less effective than previously thought.

Second, the United States might seek ways of demonstrating that it is not as highly dependent on satellite-enabled warfare as Beijing has come to believe in recent years. As discussed above, China assesses that U.S. satellites were an essential enabler of Washington's successful joint military operations against Iraq. In order to modify Chinese perceptions that the United States is heavily reliant on space and therefore reduce Beijing's focus on space deterrence, Washington could publicly reveal new capabilities outside of the space domain, such as advanced

---

[1]   DoD, 2020a, p. 2.

[2]   DoD, 2020b, p. 11.

[3]   See, for example, statements in an interview with Gen. James Dickinson, commander of U.S. Space Command, as reported in Erwin, 2021b.

surveillance remote piloted vehicles or new communications systems, which demonstrate redundancy of its space-based capabilities. Developing and messaging the existence of this redundancy could encourage China to reconsider the value of taking escalatory steps in space. From this perspective, the establishment of USSF is counterproductive because the new service implies that Beijing is correct—that is, that the United States does highly value outer space and must defend it at all costs to avoid vulnerabilities on Earth. USSF Chief of Space Operations' guidance says as much: "Space is a vital national interest. Activities on land, at sea, in the air, through cyberspace, and in the electromagnetic spectrum all depend on space superiority. The nation established the United States Space Force to ensure freedom of action for the United States in, from, and to space."[4] Chinese observers have also accurately identified the rationale behind the establishment of USSF, with one noting that "the U.S. military believes that entering, utilizing and controlling space is of great strategic significance for maintaining national defense security. The United States military has been committed to innovating tactics and strategies to control space power, strengthening the support of space organization system to ensure the technical advantages of space equipment."[5] This is not to say, however, that the establishment of USSF is an error or is somehow misguided. But the fact of USSF's existence does perhaps unavoidably show just how important defending space is for the United States and thereby confirms the Chinese approach.

Third, the United States would probably benefit from encouraging China to question its own ability to leverage the space domain in support of the PLA's system-of-systems concept of modern warfare and terrestrial-based joint operations. This might be accomplished via a demonstration of capabilities that would compromise PLA space systems, perhaps through enhanced U.S. cyberhacking, spoofing, jamming, or other dazzling capabilities against China, but could also include kinetic options as well. If Beijing believes its ability to leverage space for terrestrial-based joint operations is no longer reliable, or less

---

[4]   DoD, 2020b, p. 11.

[5]   Li, Yao, and Cui, 2019, p. 15.

reliable than previously assessed, then it might have to look elsewhere to achieve these capabilities. In this scenario, the United States may observe a reduction in China's emphasis on achieving space supremacy and its corresponding deterrence activities in space. Beijing might be compelled to cede gains toward space superiority in favor of gains in more advantageous domains. In this regard, the establishment of USSF serves the very important purpose of keeping pressure on China in space. From a Chinese perspective, it is worrying that the United States *Defense Space Strategy* calls for "build[ing] a comprehensive military advantage in space" by "building capabilities to counter hostile uses of space." The strategy further states that "DoD [will develop an agile space enterprise that can take advantage of emerging technological and commercial innovation in order to continually outpace adversary threats."[6] Beijing is undoubtedly concerned about USSF's long-term plans. There is the possibility that the United States eventually outcompetes China in space, which would ultimately prompt China to back down. Threats to outspend Moscow during the Cold War and how this strategy contributed to the Soviet Union's demise is an intriguing and relatively recent historical analogy. However, one Chinese article also highlights the destabilizing effect of USSF, noting that "the United States' increased space deterrence not only directly poses a clear threat to its opponents, but also causes international space security to increasingly slip into an arms race and security dilemma. This change at the level of the international system caused by the United States' pursuit of space hegemony has in turn shaped the current space security relationship, prompting other countries to make complex responses including counter-deterrence under system pressure."[7] Thus, USSF deterrence activities may have to be carefully calibrated to mitigate concern about its role. Messaging about USSF could emphasize its role in maintaining equitable access to space or resilience and reconstitution capabilities that deny PLA successes in space rather than simply ramping up punitive capabilities that can be mirrored on the other side.

---

[6] DoD, 2020a, p. 7.

[7] Xu and Gao, 2020.

Fourth, and finally, the United States might want to consider the nature of its deterrence messaging to China in space. As mentioned above, Washington would likely benefit from increased clarity in its warnings and intentions, signaling to Beijing that the United States will not "submit to the deterrer's volition" as China moves up its space-deterrence escalation ladder. There is a move in the space community away from technical warnings based on easily measurable metrics such as vicinity constraints in favor of behavior-based warnings, and messaging to China would benefit from following this shift. For example, the United Nations General Assembly recently passed a resolution drafted by the United Kingdom that focuses on such a behavior-based approach rather than an object-based approach.[8] The resolution, "Reducing Space Threats Through Norms, Rules, and Principles of Responsible Behaviors," gives states the flexibility to assess threats from their own national security perspective rather than presenting a unilateral assessment of threat based on an object itself. The focus of this resolution on building norms and establishing an international code of conduct is in contrast to an object-based approach that would seek a treaty that bans specific kinds of ASAT tests. This shift toward a focus on behavioral norms is a positive step toward building a deterrence strategy with effective redlines.[9] It is also the current position of the U.S. Department of State that behaviors should be the driver of deterrence messaging rather than technology and technical limits on its use.[10] The implication would be that if China does not follow acceptable behavioral norms, then negative consequences could follow. This approach could accomplish two things. First, Beijing might be less likely to place counterspace assets just beyond Washington's minimum standoff distance from the United States, thereby providing the United States with more reaction time in the event of attacks. And second, it would put the onus

---

[8] For a discussion on the U.N. General Assembly and past resolutions on arms race and security in outer space, see Krepon, 2014, or Ortega, 2021.

[9] According to space policy expert Peter Marquez, for example, the United States should shift away from vicinity-based warnings in favor of behavior-based warnings (which may be conveyed publicly or privately). See Marquez, 2011.

[10] See Ford, 2020, for statements regarding the establishment of behavioral norms.

on China to be a more responsible power in space. Heeding Marquez's advice to shift away from vicinity-based warnings in favor of behavior-based warnings could make *space force deployments*, the third rung on the Chinese space escalation ladder, fraught with greater risk to China. At present, China seems to have more of an appreciation for vicinity-based messaging, as in the U.S. delineation of specific locations as redlines, as it typically loiters in the standoff threshold. Beijing typically disregards behavior-based messaging. The shift in the international space community toward establishing norms of behavior, coupled with a shift in Washington toward behavior-based messaging, may serve to increase the perceived importance of behavior-based messaging in Beijing's mind by presenting them with increased costs should they violate these norms. Additionally, by placing the onus on China to act responsibly in space through threat of punishment or denial, this behavior-based messaging would in effect challenge Beijing's objective to "seize the initiative" early to win in space. The United States has noted China's inconsistency in its words and deeds in space, and this inconsistency is facilitated by the absence of behavioral-based norms in space.[11] China routinely advocates the peaceful use of space and use of military force for defensive purposes only, yet continues the development and testing of counterspace weapons. Widespread adoption of international norms of behavior may resonate in China and, hopefully, keep Beijing true to its words (not deeds) and compel it to change its behavior going forward.[12]

---

[11] China has asserted that the creation of the USSF is in itself an aggressive action, potentially as a means of legitimizing their own activity in space. This highlights that the United States and allies will need to carefully consider which actions of their own are to be messaged as acceptable behavior, not just the actions of China.

[12] For a recent example of China stating it intends to keep space peaceful, see Chinese Ministry of Foreign Affairs, 2020. Regarding China's defensive military strategy, it is known as "active defense." Active defense prioritizes the deployment of offensive and defensive forces and systems to extend China's defensive perimeter. Authoritative Chinese documents on active defense are explored in Heath, 2016, pp. 18–19.

CHAPTER SIX

United States Coordination with Allies and Partners

Successful deterrence against Chinese activities in space may be reinforced by involving key U.S. allies and partners. There are several allies and partners in the Indo-Pacific with shared concerns of China's growing military space capabilities, including India, Japan, South Korea, and Taiwan.

Of these allies and partners, Japan is unique because it is probably the most concerned and because it possesses the technical wherewithal in space to compete with China. Although domestic laws severely restrict Japan's ability to leverage space for military purposes, through the passage of the Basic Space Law in 2008 Tokyo was granted new authorities to engage in space activities that support Japan's national security. Since then, Japan has been steadily increasing its military presence in space. In January 2017, for example, Tokyo launched its first military communications satellite.[1] In November 2020, Tokyo launched an optical data relay satellite for both civilian and military purposes.[2] Japan is also planning to expand its intelligence, surveillance, and reconnaissance capabilities, stating in its most recent space implementation plan an expansion of the Information Gathering Satellites network of reconnaissance satellites; such capabilities could facilitate increased allied coverage of China.[3]

---

[1] Reuters Staff, 2017.

[2] "Japan Launches Data Relay Satellite to Improve Disaster Response," 2020.

[3] Japan Cabinet Office, 2017; provisional/tentative translation.

Japan is still relatively new to treating space as a military domain. The official Japanese 2020 defense white paper lists it as one of the "new domains," and Tokyo's current presence there is overwhelmingly civilian.[4] But with the passage of each milestone, Japan's threat perceptions in space have grown as well. Significantly, the defense white paper notes that "in the security area, major countries have been making proactive efforts to use outer space for maintaining peace and safety." However, the paper added, "The development and verification test of a killer satellite [country undisclosed], which approaches a target satellite to disturb, attack, and capture it, is underway, increasing the threat to the stable use of outer space."[5]

Tokyo's evolving security concerns in space have prompted Japanese strategic thinkers to consider how their country, in conjunction with their top security ally in the United States, might effectively deter China in space.[6] This strategic thinking includes a focus on a tailored deterrence approach as well as the use of cross-domain deterrence and strong partnerships to contend with China's growing military power.[7] One scholar, in considering the problem of China's growing power, concludes that "Tokyo and Washington should work together to develop a joint, cross-domain allied space deterrence strategy" and argues that a U.S.-Japan alliance should aim to enhance space deterrence by increasing the perceived cost of attacks against allied space assets and improving the resilience of space systems.[8] A partnership could strengthen behavioral norms and thereby increase the perceived cost for violating these norms. A partnership could also enhance resilience insofar as each member has shared or redundant capabilities.

---

[4] Japanese Ministry of Defense, 2020.

[5] Japanese Ministry of Defense, 2020, p. 11.

[6] One Japanese strategic thinker at the Air Command and Staff College within the Japanese Ministry of Defense, Captain Hiroshi Nakatani, is weighing the applicability of a tailored deterrence approach, implicitly to contend with China's growing military power. See Nakatani, forthcoming.

[7] One such partnership is the space situational awareness sharing agreement with the United States, in place since 2013. See DoD, 2015.

[8] Kazuto Suzuki, 2017, p. 92.

Although these initial proposals are promising, Japanese thought leaders are apparently yet to attempt to build a tailored approach to deterring China in space—whether through the alliance or independently. However, the view that Tokyo must recognize the cross-domain impacts of space deterrence is essential when considering China's military strategy of intimidation in space. Like the United States, Japan will want to ensure that it does not "submit to the deterrer's volition" because of one or several Chinese space activities. Indeed, the U.S.-Japan alliance itself bolsters both countries' resolve to *not* submit to China. This is a good thing. In terms of a Western-style deterrence strategy by punishment and denial, both punishment and denial capabilities can deter China in space, but punishment capabilities run a greater risk of causing a destabilizing arms race. Hence, Japan might consult with the United States on prioritizing denial over punitive capabilities to avoid unnecessarily worsening its space security environment.

CHAPTER SEVEN

Areas for Future Research

The purpose of this research report is to describe the key components of a deterrence strategy in space and begin the process of building a tailored deterrence profile against China in the space domain. It is clear that understanding Chinese goals in space and its approach to deterrence from space can provide U.S. decisionmakers and planners with important insights into how best to counter Beijing's approach. The use of primary source documents to characterize these goals and strategies can help to build this understanding. However, much is left to explore. While this report examines Chinese goals in the space domain and how that impacts the development of an effective deterrence strategy, it does not explore how China's space programs are being employed to achieve its goals. Future research should focus on this issue as well. Developing a richer view of Chinese perceptions and activities in space would contribute greatly to building a more nuanced approach to deterrence. Follow-on research activities should seek to glean additional insights from interviews with government officials (U.S., Chinese, Japanese, and others) and other experts. Finally, research on U.S. allies and partners' potential roles in deterrence efforts against China in space deserves greater attention in future studies. A focal point of these assessments should be the extent to which U.S. allies and partners properly understand Chinese goals and strategy in space so as to develop the most effective response.

References

Academy of Military Sciences, *The Science of Military Strategy*, eds. Peng Guangqian and Yao Youzhi, trans. Pan Jiabin, et al., Beijing: Military Science Publishing House, 2005.

Ashley, Lt. Gen. Robert, opening keynote address at CyberSat19 Summit, Reston, Va., November 7, 2019.

Astorino-Courtois, Allison, "Space and U.S. Deterrence: A Virtual Think Tank Report," National Security Institute, produced in support of the Strategic Multilayer Assessment Office, December 2017.

Brodie, Bernard, "The Absolute Weapon: Atomic Power and World Order," New Haven, Conn.: Yale Institute of International Studies, 1946.

Bunn, M. Elaine, "Can Deterrence Be Tailored?" *Strategic Forum*, No. 225, January 2007, pp. 1–8.

Cheng, Dean, "Chinese Views on Deterrence," *Joint Forces Quarterly*, No. 60, 2011, pp. 92–94.

———, "Space and Information Warfare: A Key Battleground for Information Dominance," in Nicholas Wright, ed., *Outer Space; Earthly Escalation? Chinese Perspectives on Space Operations and Escalation*, Strategic Multilayer Assessment Periodic Publication, Department of Defense and Joint Chiefs, August 2018. As of April 27, 2021:
https://nsiteam.com/social/wp-content/uploads/2018/08/SMA-White-Paper_Chinese-Persepectives-on-Space_-Aug-2018.pdf

China National Space Administration, "White Paper on China's Space Activities in 2016," People's Republic of China State Council Information Office, December 27, 2016. As of April 27, 2021:
http://www.spaceref.com/news/viewsr.html?pid=49722

China's State Council Information Office, "China's Military Strategy," Beijing, May 2015. As of April 27, 2021:
http://english.gov.cn/archive/white_paper/2015/05/27/content_281475115610833.htm

Chinese Ministry of Foreign Affairs, "China Says It's Devoted to Peaceful Use of Space," December 7, 2020, As of May 18, 2021: https://www.youtube.com/watch?v=fbLCZ1QucJs

Costello, John, and Joe McReynolds, "China's Strategic Support Force: A Force for a New Era," Washington, D.C.: Institute for National Strategic Studies, National Defense University, 2018.

DoD—*See* U.S. Department of Defense.

Engstron, Jeffrey, *Systems Confrontation and System Destruction Warfare: How the Chinese People's Liberation Army Seeks to Wage Modern Warfare*, Santa Monica, Calif.: RAND Corporation, RR-1708-OSD, 2018. As of April 26, 2021: https://www.rand.org/pubs/research_reports/RR1708.html

Erwin, Sandra, "Air Force: SSA Is No More; It's 'Space Domain Awareness,'" *Space News*, November 14, 2019. As of April 28, 2021: https://spacenews.com/air-force-ssa-is-no-more-its-space-domain-awareness/

———, "Space Surveillance Technologies a Top Need for U.S. Military," *Space News*, November 22, 2020. As of April 28, 2021: https://spacenews.com/space-surveillance-technologies-a-top-need-for-u-s-military/

———, "Space Force Needs Sensors to Distinguish Weapons from Benign Objects," *Space News*, January 6, 2021a. As of April 28, 2021: https://spacenews.com/space-force-needs-sensors-to-distinguish-weapons-from -benign-objects

———, "Dickinson's Guidance to Space Troops: Prepare for 'Competitive and Dangerous' Environment," *Space News*, January 28, 2021b. As of April 28, 2021: https://spacenews.com/dickinsons-guidance-to-space-troops-prepare-for-competitive -and-dangerous-environment/

Finch, James P., and Shawn Steene, "Finding Space in Deterrence: Toward a General Framework for 'Space Deterrence,'" *Strategic Studies Quarterly*, Vol. 10, 2011, pp. 10–17.

Ford, Christopher, "Strategic Stability and the Global Race for Technology Leadership," *Arms Control and International Security Papers*, Vol. 1, No. 21, 2020, pp. 1–9. As of May 20, 2021: https://www.state.gov/wp-content/uploads/2020/11/T-paper-series-Strategic -Stability-and-Tech-508.pdf

George, Alexander L., and Richard Smoke, *Deterrence in American Foreign Policy: Theory and Practice*, New York: Columbia University Press, 1974.

George, Justin Paul, "History of Anti-Satellite Weapons: US Tested First ASAT Missile 60 Years Ago," *The Week*, March 27, 2019.

Glaser, Charles L., *Analyzing Strategic Nuclear Policy*, Princeton, N.J.: Princeton University Press, 1990.

Gleason, Michael P., and Peter L. Hays, "Getting the Most Deterrent Value from U.S. Space Forces," Space Agenda 2021, Center for Space Policy and Strategy, Aerospace Corporation, October 27, 2020.

Grossman, Derek, "Envisioning a 'World Class' PLA: Implications for the United States and the Indo-Pacific," statement for the Record for the U.S.-China Economic and Security Review Commission, CT-514, July 1, 2019. As of April 26, 2021: https://www.rand.org/pubs/testimonies/CT514.html

Gruss, Mike, "Space Surveillance Sats Pressed into Early Service," *Space News*, September 18, 2015.

Harrison, Todd, Kaitlyn Johnson, Thomas G. Roberts, Tyler Way, and Makena Young, "Space Threat Assessment 2020," CSIS Aerospace Security Project, March 2020. As of April 27, 2021: https://aerospace.csis.org/space-threat-assessment-2020/

Heath, Timothy R., "An Overview of China's National Military Strategy," in Joe McReynolds, ed., *China's Evolving Military Strategy*, Washington, D.C.: Jamestown Foundation, 2016, pp. 18–19. As of April 27, 2021: https://jamestown.org/product/chinas-evolving-military-strategy-edited-joe-mcreynolds/

Herz, J., "Idealist Internationalism and the Security Dilemma," *World Politics,* Vol. 2, No. 2, 1950, pp. 157–180.

Japan Cabinet Office, Section 4, "Implementation Plan of the Basic Plan on Space Policy," December 12, 2017. As of June 9, 2021: https://www8.cao.go.jp/space/english/basicplan/2017/basicplan.pdf

"Japan Launches Data Relay Satellite to Improve Disaster Response," *Nikkei Asia*, November 29, 2020. As of May 18, 2021: https://asia.nikkei.com/Business/Aerospace-Defense/Japan-launches-data-relay-satellite-to-improve-disaster-response

Japanese Ministry of Defense, "Defense of Japan 2020," annual white paper, 2020. As of May 18, 2021: https://www.mod.go.jp/en/publ/w_paper/index.html

Jervis, Robert, *Perception and Misperception in International Politics*, Princeton, N.J.: Princeton University Press, 1976, pp. 62–76.

———, "Cooperation Under the Security Dilemma," *World Politics*, Vol. 30, No. 2, 1978, pp. 167–214.

Jiang Lianju and Wang Liwen, eds., *Textbook for the Study of Space Operations* [空间作战学教程], Beijing: Military Science Publishing House, 2013.

Joint Chiefs of Staff, "Joint Doctrine Note 2-19," Washington, D.C., December 10, 2019.

Kahn, Herman, *On Thermonuclear War*, Princeton, N.J.: Princeton University Press, 1961.

Kaufmann, William W., "The Requirements of Deterrence," in P. Bobbitt, L. Freeman, and G. F. Treverton, eds., *U.S. Nuclear Strategy*, London: Palgrave Macmillan, 1989. This chapter was originally sourced from W. W. Kaufmann, ed., *Military Policy and National Security*, Port Washington, N.Y.: Kennikat Press, 1972.

Kent, Glenn A., and David E. Thaler, *First-Strike Stability: A Methodology for Evaluating Strategic Forces*, Santa Monica, Calif.: RAND Corporation, R-3765-AF, 1989. As of April 26, 2021:
https://www.rand.org/pubs/reports/R3765.html

Kramer, Miriam, "Russia and China Want to Build a Moon Station Together," *Axios* (Science), March 9, 2021. As of May 20, 2021:
https://www.axios.com/Russia-china-moon-research-station-plans-f3504927-e9ed
-4921-b7f9-7f430cb93aa7.html

Krepon, Michael, "Norm-Setting for Outer Space," *Arms Control Wonk*, September 9, 2014. As of April 28, 2021:
https://www.armscontrolwonk.com/archive/404264/norm-setting-for-outer-space/

Kydd, Andrew H., *Trust and Mistrust in International Relations*, Princeton, N.J.: Princeton University Press, 2005.

Lewis, James, "'Bottom Line Thinking' About the 'Commanding Heights,'" in Nicholas Wright, ed., *Outer Space; Earthly Escalation? Chinese Perspectives on Space Operations and Escalation*, Strategic Multilayer Assessment Periodic Publication, Department of Defense and Joint Chiefs, August 2018, pp. 20–24. As of April 27, 2021:
https://nsiteam.com/social/wp-content/uploads/2018/08/SMA-White-Paper_Chinese
-Persepectives-on-Space_-Aug-2018.pdf.

Li, Hongjun, Yao Wenduo, and Cui Shuai Hao, "Main Features of U.S. Space Force Construction," Aerospace Engineering University, Beijing, Article No. 1672-8211, December 2019. As of May 18, 2021:
https://tow.cnki.net/kcms/detail/detail.aspx?filename=JSYC201904003&dbcode
=CRJT_CJFD&dbname=CJFDLAST2020&v=

Long, Austin, *Deterrence—From Cold War to Long War: Lessons from Six Decades of RAND Research*, Santa Monica, Calif.: RAND Corporation, MG-636-OSD/AF, 2008. As of April 26, 2021:
https://www.rand.org/pubs/monographs/MG636.html

Lopez, C. Todd, "Space Force Chief: U.S. Doesn't Want War in Space, Must Be Prepared for It," *Defense News*, September 15, 2020. As of May 13, 2021:
https://www.defense.gov/Explore/News/Article/Article/2348614/space-force-chief
-us-doesnt-want-war-in-space-must-be-prepared-for-it/

"Make China a Global Space Giant: Xi Jinping," *Economic Times*, April 24, 2016. As of May 13, 2021:
https://economictimes.indiatimes.com/news/international/world-news/make-china-a-global-space-giant-xi-jinping/articleshow/51967279.cms

Manzo, Vincent, "Deterrence and Escalation in Cross-Domain Operations: Where Do Space and Cyberspace Fit?" Washington, D.C.: The Center for Strategic Research, Institute for National Strategic Studies, National Defense University, December 2011.

Marquez, Peter, "Space Deterrence: The Prêt-á-Porter Suit for the Naked Emperor," in *Returning to Fundamentals: Deterrence and U.S. National Security in the 21st Century*, Washington, D.C.: The George Marshall Institute, 2011.

Mayfield, Mandy, "Space Commander Warns Chinese Lasers Could Blind US Satellites," *National Defense*, September 27, 2019. As of May 13, 2021:
https://www.nationaldefensemagazine.org/articles/2019/9/27/space-commander-warns-chinese-lasers-could-blind-us-satellites

Mazarr, Michael J., *Understanding Deterrence*, Santa Monica, Calif.: RAND Corporation, PE-295-RC, 2018. As of May 13, 2021:
https://www.rand.org/pubs/perspectives/PE295.html

Morgan, Forrest E., *Deterrence and First Strike Stability in Space: A Preliminary Assessment*, Santa Monica, Calif.: RAND Corporation, MG-916-AF, 2010. As of April 26, 2021:
https://www.rand.org/pubs/monographs/MG916.html

Morgan, P. M., *Deterrence Now*, Cambridge Studies in International Relations series, 89, New York: Cambridge University Press, 2003.

Mueller, Karl P., "The Absolute Weapon and the Ultimate High Ground: Why Nuclear Deterrence and Space Deterrence Are Strikingly Similar—Yet Profoundly Different," in Michael Krepon and Julia Thompson, eds., *Anti-Satellite Weapons, Deterrence and Sino-American Space Relations*, Washington, D.C.: Stimson Center, September 2013.

Mueller, Karl P., Jasen J. Castillo, Forrest E. Morgan, Negeen Pegahi, and Brian Rosen, *Striking First: Preemptive and Preventive Attack in U.S. National Security Policy*, Santa Monica, Calif.: RAND Corporation, MG-403-AF, 2006. As of April 27, 2021:
https://www.rand.org/pubs/monographs/MG403.html

Mutschler, Max M., *Arms Control in Space: Exploring Conditions for Preventive Arms Control*, London: Palgrave Macmillan, 2013.

Nakatani, Hiroshi, "The Validity and Limitations of Tailored Deterrence," JASDF Command and Staff College, forthcoming.

Ortega, Almudena Azcárate, "Placement of Weapons in Outer Space: The Dichotomy Between Word and Deed," *Lawfare Blog*, January 28, 2021. As of April 28, 2021: https://www.lawfareblog.com/placement-weapons-outer-space-dichotomy-between -word-and-deed

Pfrang, Kaila, and Brian Weeden, "U.S. Military and Intelligence Rendezvous and Proximity Operations in Space," Broomfield, Colo.: Secure World Foundation, August 2020.

Pollpeter, Kevin, Eric Anderson, Jordan Wilson, and Fan Yang, *China Dream, Space Dream: China's Progress in Space Technologies and Implications for the United States*, Washington, D.C.: U.S. Economic and Security Review Commission, 2015. As of April 27, 2021: https://www.uscc.gov/sites/default/files/Research/China%20Dream%20Space %20Dream_Report.pdf

Pollpeter, Kevin L., Michael S. Chase, and Eric Heginbotham, *The Creation of the PLA Strategic Support Force and Its Implications for Chinese Military Space Operations*, Santa Monica, Calif.: RAND Corporation, RR-2058-AF, 2017. As of April 26, 2021: https://www.rand.org/pubs/research_reports/RR2058.html

Reuters Staff, "Japan Launches First Military Communications Satellite," *Reuters*, January 24, 2017. As of May 18, 2021: https://www.reuters.com/article/us-japan-military-satellite/japan-launches-first -military-communications-satellite-idUSKBN1580VZ

Schelling, T. C., *The Strategy of Conflict*, Cambridge, Mass.: Harvard University Press, 1960.

———, *Arms and Influence*. New Haven, Conn.: Yale University Press, 1966, pp. 187–203.

Shelton, Gen. William L., "Threats to Space Assets and Implications for Homeland Security," Statement to House Armed Services Subcommittee on Strategic Forces and House Homeland Security Subcommittee on Emergency Preparedness, Response and Communication, March 29, 2017.

Sigal, Leon V., "Stability and Reduction of Nuclear Forces: The Intercontinental and Theater Levels," *Bulletin of Peace Proposals*, Vol. 16, No. 3, 1985, pp. 233–239.

Snyder, Glenn H., *Deterrence by Denial and Punishment*, Princeton, N.J.: Center of International Studies, January 1959.

———, "Deterrence and Power," *Journal of Conflict Resolution*, Vol. 4, No. 2, 1960, pp. 163–178.

State Council Information Office of the People's Republic of China, "China's National Defense in the New Era," Beijing, July 2019. As of April 27, 2021: https://www.andrewerickson.com/2019/07/full-text-of-defense-white-paper-chinas -national-defense-in-the-new-era-english-chinese-versions/

Stokes, Mark, Gabriel Alvarado, Emily Weinstein, and Ian Easton, *China's Space and Counterspace Capabilities and Activities*, prepared for the U.S.-China Economic and Security Review Commission, Arlington, Va.: Project 2049 Institute and Pointe Bello, March 30, 2020. As of April 27, 2021:
https://www.uscc.gov/sites/default/files/2020-05/China_Space_and_Counterspace
_Activities.pdf

Sun Haiyang and Chang Jinan, "A New Shape of Military Deterrence—Space Deterrence," *Military Art*, Vol. 10, 2003.

Suzuki, Kazuto, "A Japanese Perspective on Space Deterrence and the Role of the U.S.-Japan Alliance in Outer Space," in Scott W. Harold, Yoshiaki Nakagawa, Junichi Fukuda, John A. Davis, Keiko Kono, Dean Cheng, and Kazuto Suzuki, *The U.S.-Japan Alliance and Deterring Gray Zone Coercion in the Maritime, Cyber, and Space Domains*, Santa Monica, Calif.: RAND Corporation, CF-379-GOJ, 2017. As of April 27, 2021:
https://www.rand.org/pubs/conf_proceedings/CF379.html

"To Counter China's Rise, the U.S. Should Focus on Ji," *Politico,* January 28, 2021. As of April 28, 2021:
https://www.politico.com/news/magazine/2021/01/28/china-foreign-policy-long
-telegram-anonymous-463120

Townsend, Lt. Col. Brad, "Strategic Choice and the Orbital Security Dilemma," *Strategic Studies Quarterly*, Spring 2020, pp. 64–90.

United Nations General Assembly, "Treaty on Principles Governing the Activities of States in the Exploration and Use of Outer Space, including the Moon and Other Celestial Bodies," Resolution 2222 (XXI) adopted January 1967. As of June 9, 2021:
https://www.unoosa.org/oosa/en/ourwork/spacelaw/treaties/outerspacetreaty.html

United Nations Office for Outer Space Affairs, "Status of International Agreements Relating to Activities in Outer Space," Vienna, April 21, 2021. As of April 28, 2021:
https://www.unoosa.org/oosa/en/ourwork/spacelaw/treaties/status/index.html

U.S.-China Economic and Security Review Commission, "2019 Report to Congress of the U.S.-China Economic and Security Review Commission," November 2019. As of April 27, 2021:
https://www.uscc.gov/annual-report/2019-annual-report-congress

U.S. Congress, H.R. 2500 National Defense Authorization Act for Fiscal Year 2020, 116th Congress, 2019–2020. As of April 27, 2021:
https://www.congress.gov/bill/116th-congress/house-bill/2500/

U.S. Defense Intelligence Agency, "Challenges to Security in Space," January 2019. As of May 13, 2021:
https://www.dia.mil/Portals/27/Documents/News/Military%20Power
%20Publications/Space_Threat_V14_020119_sm.pdf

U.S. Department of Defense, "The Guidelines for U.S.-Japan Defense Cooperation," Washington, D.C., April 27, 2015.

―――, *Defense Space Strategy Summary*, Washington, D.C., June 2020a. As of May 13, 2021:
https://media.defense.gov/2020/Jun/17/2002317391/-1/-1/1/2020_DEFENSE _SPACE_STRATEGY_SUMMARY.PDF

―――, *Chief of Space Operations' Planning Guidance*, 1st Chief of Space Operation, November 9, 2020b. As of April 27:
https://media.defense.gov/2020/Nov/09/2002531998/-1/-1/0/CSO%20PLANNING %20GUIDANCE.PDF

U.S. National Academy of Sciences and Chinese People's Association for Peace and Disarmament, *English-Chinese Chinese-English Nuclear Security Glossary*, Washington, D.C.: National Academies Press, 2008.

U.S. Office of Space Commerce, *National Space Policy of the United States of America*, December 9, 2020, pp. 3–4.

U.S. Space Command Public Affairs Office, "Russia Conducts Space-Based Anti-Satellite Weapons Test," July 23, 2020a. As of May 20, 2021:
https://www.spacecom.mil/MEDIA/NEWS-ARTICLES/Article/2285098/russia -conducts-space-based-anti-satellite-weapons-test/

―――, "Russia Tests Direct-Ascent Anti-Satellite Missile," U.S. Space Command Public Affairs Office, December 16, 2020b. As of May 20, 2021:
https://www.spacecom.mil/News/Article-Display/Article/2448334/russia-tests -direct-ascent-anti-satellite-missile/

Van Evera, Stephen, "Offense, Defense, and the Causes of War," *International Security*, Vol. 22, No. 4, Spring 1998, pp. 5–43.

Vasani, Harsh, "How China is Weaponizing Outer Space," *The Diplomat*, January 19, 2017. As of May 13, 2021:
https://thediplomat.com/2017/01/how-china-is-weaponizing-outer-space/

Vergun, David, "Space Domain Critical to Combat Operations Since Desert Storm," *DoD News*, March 19, 2021. As of May 13, 2021:
https://www.defense.gov/Explore/News/Article/Article/2543941/space-domain -critical-to-combat-operations-since-desert-storm/

Wohlstetter, Albert, *The Delicate Balance of Terror*, Santa Monica, Calif.: RAND Corporation, P-1472, 1958. As of April 26, 2021:
https://www.rand.org/pubs/papers/P1472.html

Xi Jinping, "Secure a Decisive Victory in Building a Moderately Prosperous Society in All Respects and Strive for the Great Success of Socialism with Chinese Characteristics for a New Era," speech at 19th Party Congress, October 18, 2017. As of April 27, 2021:
http://www.chinadaily.com.cn/china/19thcpcnationalcongress/2017-11/04/ content_34115212.htm

Xin Dingding, "Space Exploration Part of the Chinese Dream," Embassy of the People's Republic of China in Ireland, June 25, 2013. As of April 27, 2021: http://ie.china-embassy.org/eng/ztlt/chinesedream/t1075175.htm

Xu Nengwu and Gao Yangyuxi, "System Pressure and Strategic Direction in the Construction of Space Security Order," *Journal of International Security Studies*, February 2020. As of May 18, 2021: http://cssn.cn/gjgxx/gj_gjgxll/202006/t20200630_5149228_1.shtml

Yanarella, Ernest, "The Missile Defense Controversy: Technology in Search of a Mission," Lexington: University Press of Kentucky, 1977.

Zagare, F., and D. Kilgour, *Perfect Deterrence*, Cambridge: Cambridge University Press, 2000.

Zhao Wentao [赵文涛] and Huang Wei [黄巍], "Abandon 'Hard Killing' and Pursue 'Little Damage': US Space Deterrence Mode Changes, Showing a Sense of Caution" ["摒弃"硬杀伤"追求"轻毁伤" 美太空威慑方式转变透出谨慎之心"], *Science and Technology Daily* [科技日报], May 13, 2020. As of April 27, 2021: http://digitalpaper.stdaily.com/http_www.kjrb.com/kjrb/html/2020-05/13/content_444676.htm?div=-1